Copyright © Joy Berry, 2020
Reprinted by permission. Originally Published 1987

The statements and opinions expressed in this work are solely those of the author and do not reflect the thoughts or opinions of the publisher.

Every effort has been made to trace the copyright holder(s) and obtain permission to reproduce all elements of this material.

All rights reserved. No part of this book may be reproduced or used in any manner without the prior written permission of the copyright owner, except for the use of brief quotations in a book review. For inquiries or to request permission, contact the publisher at rights@lemurpress.com

ISBN 978-1-63617-031-2

Published by Lemur Press
lemurpress.com

LEMUR PRESS

Now that I am older,
I go to preschool.

I love preschool.

I have a teacher at my school.

My teacher takes care of me, and teaches me new things.

I love my teacher.

There are other children at my school.

We play, work, and learn together.

I love the children at my preschool.

I have a classroom at my preschool.

There is a special place for me to put my belongings.

There are many fun activities for me to do in my classroom.

Sometimes I sit in a chair and do activities at a table.

Sometimes I do activities on a rug or on the floor.

I have a play yard at my school.

There are many fun things for me to use in the play yard.

There are many things for me to do.

There is a place for me to eat and drink at my school.

There is a place for me to rest.

There is a place for me to go to the bathroom at my school.

There is a place for me to wash my hands.

I have friends at my school.

We make and do many things together.

I love preschool!

www.ingramcontent.com/pod-product-compliance
Lightning Source LLC
Chambersburg PA
CBHW081413070526
44583CB00020B/2787